Who Needs an ICEBERG?

An Arctic Ecosystem

KAREN PATKAU

TUNDRA BOOKS

Published in Canada by Tundra Books,
75 Sherbourne Street, Toronto, Ontario M5A 2P9

Published in the United States by Tundra Books of Northern New York,
P.O. Box 1030, Plattsburgh, New York 12901

Library of Congress Control Number: 2011923285

Library and Archives Canada Cataloguing in Publication

Patkau, Karen
    Who needs an iceberg? : an Arctic ecosystem / by Karen Patkau.

(Ecosystem series)
ISBN 978-0-88776-993-1

    1. Ecology – Arctic regions – Juvenile literature. 2. Arctic regions – Juvenile
literature. I. Title. II. Series: Ecosystem series

QH84.1.P38 2012   j577.09719   C2011-901377-0

We acknowledge the financial support of the Government of Canada through
the Book Publishing Industry Development Program (BPIDP) and that of the
Government of Ontario through the Ontario Media Development Corporation's
Ontario Book Initiative. We further acknowledge the support of the Canada
Council for the Arts and the Ontario Arts Council for our publishing program.

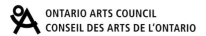

ONTARIO ARTS COUNCIL
CONSEIL DES ARTS DE L'ONTARIO

Medium: Digital

Design: Karen Patkau
Typesetting: Leah Springate

Printed and bound in China

1 2 3 4 5 6   17 16 15 14 13 12

To Dr. Jane Berg,

with special thanks to my family and friends.

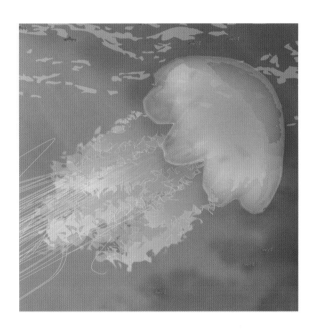

WELCOME TO THE ARCTIC

On top of the world lies an ice-covered ocean, surrounded by frozen land. Northern lights flash and swirl across the night sky.

Farthest north are ice sheets and glaciers, thousands of years old. They blanket mountains, plains, and islands.

Winter blasts snow across the open flat tundra. Spring's sunshine warms up the land. Summer bursts with life. Fall brings freezing temperatures again.

This is a vast cold place. Living conditions are extreme. From the North Pole to the tree line, this is the Arctic.

HOW AN ICEBERG FORMS

As snow and ice crystals pile up and pack down, thick dense ice sheets develop.

Glaciers are ice sheets that flow very slowly over the ground. When they reach the ocean, huge chunks break off into the water. Pieces of coastal ice break off, too. These frozen freshwater masses are icebergs.

The magnificent peak, appearing to float on the surface, is only the "tip of the iceberg." Nine-tenths of it looms below.

When an iceberg drifts to a mild climate, it melts. Hear it pop, crack, and fizzle as ancient trapped air escapes.

SOIL LAYERS

◄ topsoil

◄ permafrost

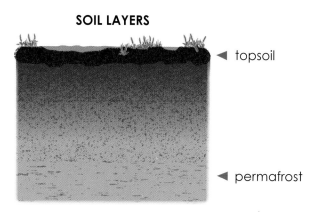

THE TUNDRA IS A DESERT

The arctic tundra is a great treeless plain. Winter is so bitterly cold that little snow falls here. Summer is cool, without much rain. The plain is an icy desert.

Below a thin layer of topsoil is permafrost – soil, frozen year-round. Trees with deep roots cannot grow here.

Bogs and pools of water sit on the dry land during summer. Water cannot sink into the solid ground.

In spite of the harsh environment, low shrubs, wildflowers, grasses, lichens, and mosses thrive.

LIVING IN THE ARCTIC

On land and in the sea, communities of living things connect with each other and their surroundings. The Arctic is an enormous ecosystem.

Let's meet some of the animals living here.

Arctic char cruise through nutrient-rich seawater. A lion's mane sea jelly pulses along. Deep below the surface swim squid and Greenland sharks.

Narwhals and beluga whales inhabit the Arctic Ocean, too.

A polar bear stalks coastal ice for ringed seal, his favorite food.

Hidden in a snow cave are a ringed seal mother and pup. Hearing his footsteps, they dive through the airhole in the shelter's ice floor and escape into the sea.

Seabirds, such as murres and puffins, plunge off cliffs and dive to great depths for fish.

Walruses haul themselves onto shore and crowd together. Noisy bullies among them wave their tusks about.

Always traveling, caribou seek pastures to graze on. A day-old calf struggles to keep up with his mother.

Arctic foxes shed thick white winter coats for thinner dark fur. Kits romp near their den while both parents hunt to feed the family.

Fluffy feathered feet help the ptarmigan walk on snow. In summer, his white feathers become mixed with brown for camouflage.

THE FOOD CHAIN

All plants and animals need energy to survive. Energy passes from one to another as food.

A food chain is created when one living thing depends on another that depends on another for food.

Plants make their own food through a process called photosynthesis. Plant-eaters are called herbivores. An arctic hare and a Dall sheep are herbivores.

Next are carnivores, like the arctic skua and the stoat. They eat other animals.

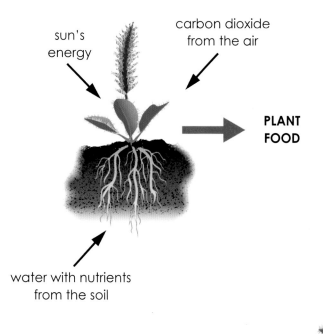

sun's energy

carbon dioxide from the air

PLANT FOOD

water with nutrients from the soil

At the base of the food chain in the sea are small aquatic life-forms called plankton.

Phytoplankton are plants the size of dust specks. Tiny animals called zooplankton eat phytoplankton.

Bigger fish and marine animals eat zooplankton. In turn, others eat some of these fish and animals.

Some land animals, including people, eat food from the sea.

PLANKTON

zooplankton

phytoplankton

krill eating plankton

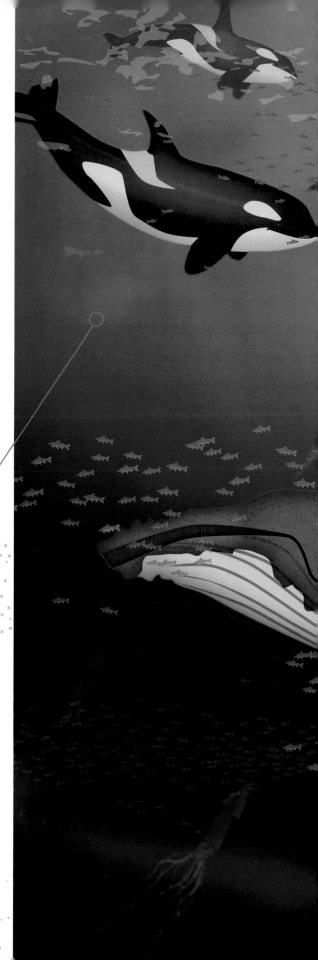

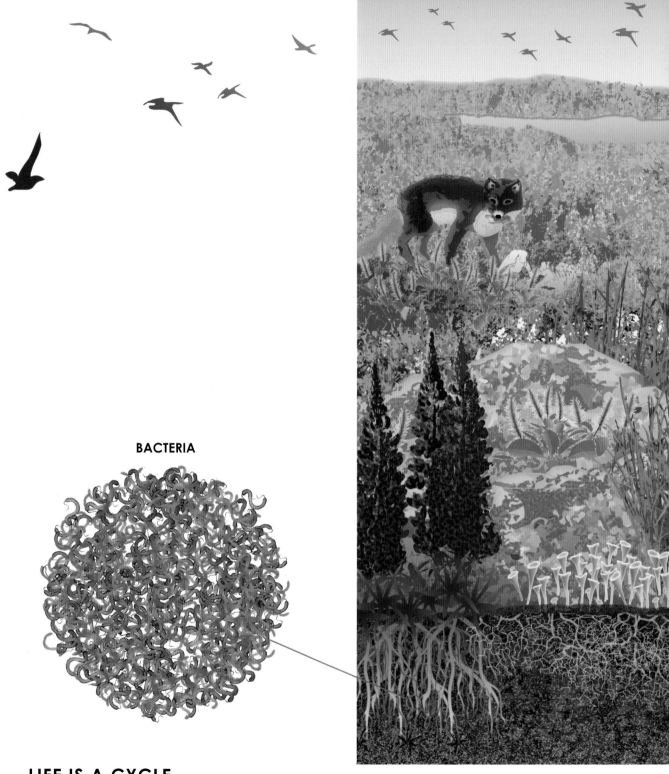

BACTERIA

LIFE IS A CYCLE

Someday all plants and animals die. Scavengers eat their remains. Decomposers recycle anything leftover.

In arctic soil, bacteria and fungi live on and decompose dead matter. They break it down into substances such as nutrients. Plants need nutrients to grow.

In the ocean, uneaten dead things sink
to the bottom and decompose. Nutrients
are released into the water. Plankton use
those carried up by water currents.

SUMMER IS A SEASON OF PLENTY

During the brief arctic summer, the sun never sets. See it in the midnight sky. Now plants grow quickly, and animals raise their young.

Millions of birds gather from all over the world. They nest on the tundra and gobble up mosquitoes, flies, and grasshoppers.

Bell heather and lupines flower between clumps of grass, arctic willows, and sedge. They are food for land animals, large and small.

Huge plankton masses bloom in the water, feeding fish and krill. Humpback and blue whales migrate from the south

Plummeting from the sky, arctic terns hunt fish in the ocean. Seals hunt fish, too. Orca whales hunt fish and seals

WINTER IS A LONG COLD NIGHT

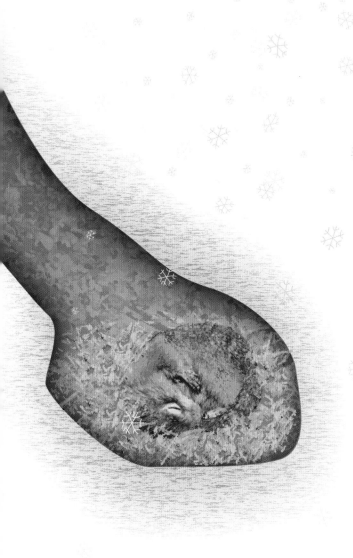

For six months, there is no daylight at the North Pole. Winter is a long dark night. Sea creatures swim in frigid black water.

Farther south, twilight glows on the tundra. The sun stays just below the horizon, while an arctic ground squirrel hibernates in his underground den.

Collared lemmings tunnel through the snow. They feed on grasses stored from summer. A hungry snowy owl hears one moving. Silently she glides over … then pounces!

Heavy-coated musk oxen do not mind blizzards. Backing into a circle, the herd fends off wolves.

WHO NEEDS AN ICEBERG?

On Earth, hot and cold times happen naturally. Since the mid-twentieth century, human activities have contributed to warmer weather.

When we burn fuel to produce electricity or run factories and machines, "greenhouse gases" are released into the air. As they increase, so does the temperature.

The Arctic is changing because of this "global warming." The Arctic Ice Cap is melting. Polar bear hunting grounds are shrinking. The home of arctic people is threatened.

As polar ice melts, weather patterns change. Sea levels rise around the world. Habitats for land animals and humans could disappear.

White ice reflects the sun's energy back into space. Without ice, dark seawater and land absorb the heat of the sun. Earth warms up even more.

Who needs an iceberg? We all do.

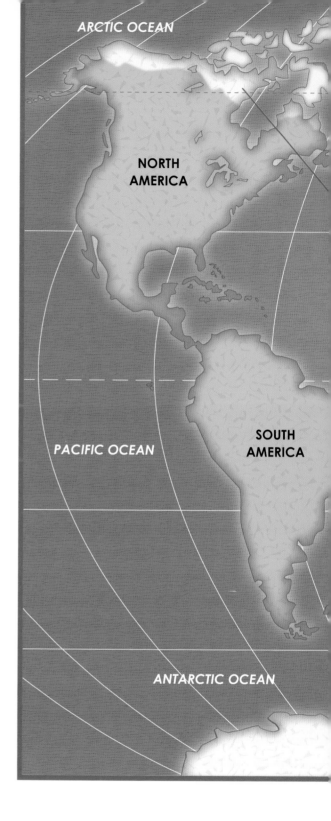

ARCTIC TUNDRA AND POLAR AREAS OF THE WORLD

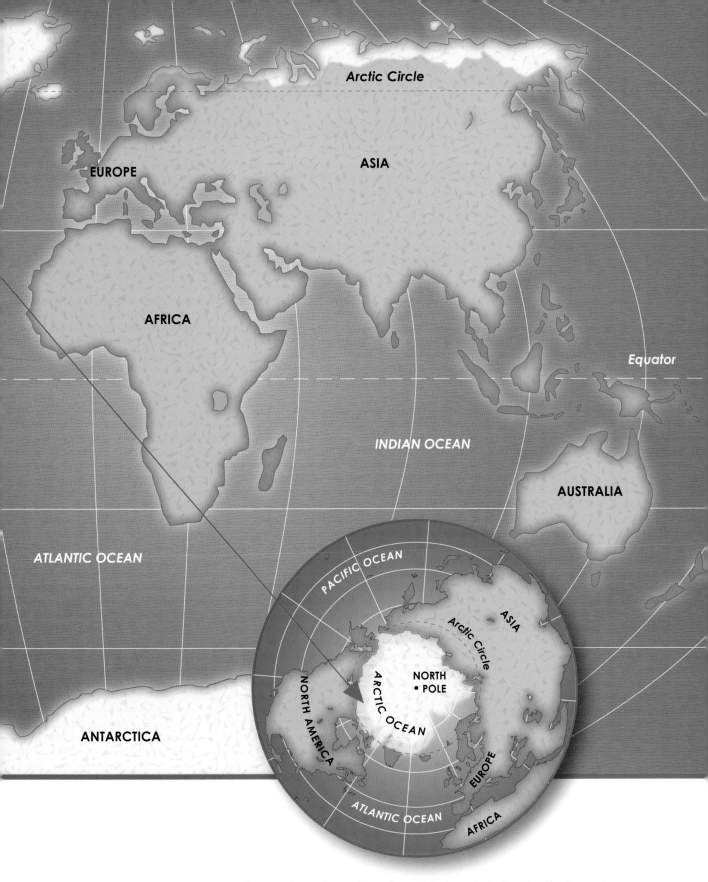

The arctic region described in this book is in North America.

HERE IS MORE INFORMATION ABOUT SOME OF THE ARCTIC INHABITANTS:

Arctic Char
These fish live in freshwater lakes and in the salty sea. No other freshwater fish are found as far north. Seawater char are larger than freshwater char.

Arctic Fox
This small fox preys on rodents, birds, and even fish. In winter, it will follow a polar bear to eat leftover scraps from its kill. Furry paws help it walk on ice.

Arctic Skua
The skua raises its young on land, but spends most of its life at sea. This hunter is also a pirate. It snatches fish from other seabirds as they fly.

Arctic Tern
Flying all the way from the Antarctic Ocean in spring, the arctic tern migrates farther than any other bird. It nests on the tundra. In fall, it returns to southern waters.

Arctic Willows
These plants are food for many tundra animals. They have flowering spikes, or catkins. Their small oval leaves are covered in tiny hairs for warmth.

Bell Heather
Bell heather is a dwarf or low-growing shrub. It has strong woody branches and tiny bell-shaped flowers. Its leaves stay green year-round.

Beluga Whale

With no dorsal fin on its back, the small white whale swims easily under ice sheets to hunt. Like all whales, it must come to the surface to breathe.

Collared Lemming

The collared lemming is the only rodent that turns white in winter. Its front feet develop two enlarged claws for burrowing through ice and snow.

Dall Sheep

Large and wild, the Dall sheep has horns that grow throughout its life. Its coat is white year-round. With flexible two-toed hooves, it dashes across steep rocky land to escape predators.

Greenland Shark

Its upper teeth are long and pointed. Its lower teeth are large and smooth. The big shark swims slowly, often at great depths, and ambushes fast-moving prey.

Krill

A small shrimplike creature, the krill is an important part of the food chain in the sea. It feeds on phytoplankton and is eaten by larger marine animals, including whales.

Lichens

Lichens are two-part organisms made up of fungi and plantlike algae. They can grow in harsh climates, on barren places such as rock and animal bone.

Lupines

Bright lupine flowers grow on stalks. Leaflets grow out from central stems. The word "lupine" comes from the Latin word *lupus*, which means wolf.

Mosses

Mosses are small plants with leafy stems that lack flowers and true roots. Clumps of moss plants grow closely together. They carpet the ground in moist shady places.

Musk Ox

This stocky plant-eater is a relative of a mountain sheep or goat. Long straight hair and an undercoat of soft wool keep it warm throughout the winter.

Narwhals

Narwhals are medium-sized toothed whales. One long spiraling tusk grows from a front tooth in the male's upper jaw. The female narwhal rarely grows a tusk.

Phytoplankton

Like plants on land, phytoplankton need sunlight, water, and nutrients to survive. They grow near the ocean's surface, where they can get the most sun.

Polar Bear

The largest land predator is on top of the arctic food chain. The creamy-white polar bear hunts seals during winter. It may go without food in summer, when coastal ice melts.

Puffin
The "sea parrot" is known for its large colorful beak. It has short wings, a stubby body and tail, and webbed feet. It can fly through the air and swim underwater.

Ringed Seal
A thick layer of blubber keeps the ringed seal warm in cold northern seawater. The seal is named for the white rings around the dark gray spots on its coat.

Sedge
A grasslike plant, sedge has a three-sided solid stem. It is common on the tundra. Herbivores eat the plant fresh or dig through winter snow and eat it frozen.

Snowy Owl
A bird of prey, the big owl is active day and night. It has excellent eyesight and hearing. Circles of feathers around its eyes reflect sound to its ears.

Stoat
The stoat or ermine is a small member of the weasel family. It makes itself at home in the rock dens or underground burrows of animals that it hunts.

Zooplankton
Zooplankton are very tiny creatures, which float freely about. They include single-celled animals, little crustaceans, and early-stage animals, such as fish, lobsters, squid, and sea jellies.

GLOSSARY

bacteria – tiny single-celled organisms that break down the remains of other living things

camouflage – to disguise something so that it appears as part of its surroundings

currents – areas of water or air flowing in a certain direction

decomposers – organisms, such as bacteria, fungi, and some types of worms, which break down dead matter

ecosystem – a community of plants, animals, and organisms that interact with each other and their physical environment. There are many different ecosystems on Earth.

environment – the surroundings and conditions in which something exists or lives

fungi – nongreen plants, such as mushrooms and molds, which live off other things

global warming – the rise in average temperature of air near the earth's surface since the mid-twentieth century

greenhouse gases – gases in the earth's atmosphere that trap heat. The main greenhouse gases are carbon dioxide, methane, and nitrous oxide.

habitats – the natural homes of plants or animals

hibernates – spends the winter in an inactive sleeplike state

migrate – to seasonally move from one place to another for feeding or breeding

North Pole – the north end of the earth's axis of rotation

northern lights – streams of colored light that appear in the northern hemisphere's night sky, also known as the aurora borealis

photosynthesis – how plants make food using energy from the sun, carbon dioxide from the air, and water

polar – found in regions near the north and south ends of the earth's axis of rotation

predators – animals that hunt other animals for food

prey – an animal that is hunted by another animal for food

sea levels – the levels of the seas' surfaces in relation to land

topsoil – the upper layer of soil that supplies plants with nourishment

tree line – the imaginary line above which no trees grow, also known as the timberline